Tim Soutphommasane is a political theorist and human rights advocate. From 2013 to 2018 he was Race Discrimination Commissioner at the Australian Human Rights Commission. His previous books include *Reclaiming Patriotism*, *The Virtuous Citizen*, *Don't Go Back to Where You Came From* and *I'm Not Racist But...* He has been a columnist for *The Age* and *The Weekend Australian*.

Writers in the *On Series*

Fleur Anderson

Gay Bilson

John Birmingham

Julian Burnside

Blanche d'Alpuget

Paul Daley

Robert Dessaix

Juliana Engberg

Sarah Ferguson

Nikki Gemmell

Stan Grant

Germaine Greer

Sarah Hanson-Young

Jonathan Holmes

Daisy Jeffrey

Susan Johnson

Malcolm Knox

Barrie Kosky

Sally McManus

David Malouf

Paula Matthewson

Katharine Murphy

Dorothy Porter

Leigh Sales

Mark Scott

Tory Shepherd

Tim Soutphommasane

David Speers

Natasha Stott Despoja

Anne Summers

Tony Wheeler

Ashleigh Wilson

Elisabeth Wynhausen

Tim Soutphommasane

On Hate

hachette
AUSTRALIA

*Every attempt has been made to locate the copyright holders for
material quoted in this book. Any person or organisation that may
have been overlooked or misattributed may contact the publisher.*

hachette
AUSTRALIA

Published in Australia and New Zealand in 2020
by Hachette Australia
(an imprint of Hachette Australia Pty Limited)
Level 17, 207 Kent Street, Sydney NSW 2000
www.hachette.com.au

First published in 2019 by Melbourne University Publishing

10 9 8 7 6 5 4 3 2 1

Copyright © Tim Soutphommasane 2019

A catalogue record for this
book is available from the
National Library of Australia

ISBN: 978 0 7336 4425 2 (paperback)

Original cover concept by Nada Backovic Design
Text design by Alice Graphics
Typeset by Typeskill
Printed and bound in Australia by McPherson's Printing Group

The paper this book is printed on is certified against the
Forest Stewardship Council® Standards. McPherson's Printing
Group holds FSC® chain of custody certification SA-COC-005379.
FSC® promotes environmentally responsible, socially beneficial
and economically viable management of the world's forests.

All of us know how to hate. But not all of us know what it's like to be hated. Few of us are ready for the experience. We enjoy being liked, better still, loved and admired. We're not programmed to enjoy scorn and rejection.

Yet it's hard to escape hate's presence in public life. Debates are becoming defined by anger, resentment and intolerance. We seem to vent rather than listen, attack rather than compromise. Those who enter the public sphere must endure not only criticism of their ideas, but also attacks on their character and identity. If you're a member of a racial minority, a woman, or have a sexual orientation other than straight, expect an extra dose of vitriol.

I've never run for public office and I've never been a politician. But for five years, while I was Race Discrimination Commissioner, there were few days when I didn't have to deal with hate. There were the incidents of racial vilification, intimidation and violence brought to my attention by members of the community. There were the racial provocations of commentators and politicians seeking to inflame public opinion. Then there was the hate directed at me, personally.

I was no stranger to hate when I took the job in 2013. Some years ago, while a columnist for *The Weekend Australian*, I received regular hate mail from readers. Outside of work, like many other Asian Australians and people of colour, I've had my experiences of racist abuse and prejudice. I've had a solid and lengthy education in how to have a thick skin.

When your mission is to fight racism, you also expect to be something of a target for bigots and extremists. I wasn't surprised when in the first weeks on the job I received an anonymous death threat in the mail: a few sheets of aggressive scrawl, accompanied by a photocopied picture of me with a noose drawn around my neck. I had been bracing for worse. I was told that one of my predecessors had been in the crosshairs of neo-Nazis some decades earlier, at one point even being exposed to a highly credible threat. The hate I experienced—typically, racist insults prompted by critical media commentary; the occasional online 'trolling' attacks launched by white supremacist groups in the United States—seemed modest by comparison.

The hate messages grew more frequent, however, amid the heated debate about the *Racial Discrimination Act 1975*. For many conservatives and libertarians on the right, the repeal of section 18C of the Racial Discrimination Act (which prohibits public acts of racial hatred) assumed the proportions of a political crusade for freedom. As one of the voices that insisted on the legislation remaining intact, I was naturally part of this contest. I regarded it my duty as Commissioner to be the guardian of the Act and to defend its integrity. Any diminution of the Act risked signalling to society that racist hate was a permissible exercise of free speech.

In 2016, I was drawn deeper into the debate, following the controversy involving a cartoon Bill Leak had drawn of a drunk Aboriginal father for *The Australian*. Some argued I had improperly solicited complaints against Leak, when I said that people who believed they experienced racial hatred had the option of making a complaint under the Racial Discrimination Act. For the campaigners against the legislation, this was proof I was a bureaucrat unjustly targeting a cartoonist for doing his job in provoking debate.

Leak himself turned his attention my way. In the space of about six months, he drew close to a dozen cartoons featuring me. One cartoon depicted me in a grotesque style as North Korean dictator Kim Jong-Un, captioned 'Tim Jong-Un'. There was the one that presented me as a brown-shirted Nazi touting for racial discrimination complaints. Another had me as a dwarf-sized North Korean army general serving a notice to the towering figure of Donald Trump.

When Leak died of a suspected heart attack in 2017, some of the media commentary suggested that I should wear the blame—that the alleged persecution of Leak, which I supposedly spearheaded at the Australian Human Rights Commission, was responsible for his death. At a memorial service for Leak at Sydney Town Hall, one man was photographed brandishing a poster with a cartoon of me and Commission president Gillian Triggs. The poster read: 'WANTED for the untimely death of Bill Leak and other crimes against Western Civilisation.'

Some time before all that, I framed a few of Leak's cartoons and put them on my office wall. One member of my staff expressed their discomfort, explaining they regarded some of Leak's cartoons to be racist in the way they caricatured me. But I wasn't too troubled about becoming an object of hate for a certain group of people. Confronted with the choice of fight or flight, I'd fight. A friend reminded me of what US president Franklin Delano Roosevelt famously said of his enemies: 'I welcome their hatred.'

I adopted it as my credo. After all, it wasn't my job to be liked or to soothe people into thinking Australia didn't have racism. If those who wished to inflict bigotry on others were directing hatred at me, presumably because I got in the way, that was to be taken as a compliment. I wasn't in it to win their approval. I was in it for the people who experienced racism, but who mightn't have the power to speak up for themselves. It was my job to speak for them, and it was my job to take the heat.

The experience of being hated wasn't one I sought, but it did focus my mind on what was at stake. Let me put it this way: You get defined in life as much by those who oppose you, as by what you stand for. If you believe in something, if you live your life with conviction, you should be comfortable about making some enemies. And you should be prepared to fight back against your haters.

Besides, not all forms of hate are to be regarded as dangerous. What's wrong with hating tyranny and injustice? What's wrong with hating bigotry and prejudice? Far from being in conflict with freedom and equality, such feelings can motivate you to right wrongs. You can hate an unjust law or an unjust system, and be moved to do something about it. You can hate what someone stands for, without succumbing to a hatred of that person or their group. You can sublimate a feeling of hatred and harness it as civic virtue.

Life also gets boring without hate. It's why utopias would be awfully monotonous places in which to live. 'Without something to hate', as the essayist William Hazlitt wrote, 'we should lose the very spring of thought and action'. Why, 'life would turn to a stagnant pool, were it not ruffled by the jarring interests, the unruly passions, of men'.[1]

Of course, there is hate and there is hate. More often than not, hate isn't used to motivate acts for the good, but acts for evil. We rightly condemn hatred directed at people because of their race, religion, sex or sexual orientation. And we rightly reject hatred, of whatever kind, that escalates to violence.

My point, though, is about how we deal with such hate. When faced with conflict, the doctrine of love seems only fit for the faint-hearted. Love isn't the simple answer, even if it makes us feel good about ourselves, or more righteous in our cause. Insisting that the light will prevail over the darkness isn't enough to make it happen. Sometimes, professing love

in the face of hate can be a sure way to guarantee defeat. Overcoming hate demands that
you be prepared for a clear-eyed confronta-
tion with reality.

In recent years, a contagion of tribalism
has infected many countries. Debates have
become increasingly polarised. Democratic
politics has grown more uncivil and punish-
ing. We're caught in a cycle of partisan nastiness. People are receiving their news and
information from sources that conform to
their worldview, and in ways that reinforce
their biases. Mutual incomprehension is
turning into mutual antagonism.

There's a particular form of hatred that
is a special problem: racism. In many ways,
racism is the prototype of hate. It combines
prejudice, discrimination and institutional

power to perpetuate racial hierarchies, which devalue some because of their background. It's also a hatred of demonstrable and horrendous evil. When carried to its ultimate conclusions, racism means systemic violence, mass murder, genocidal extermination.

For all the progress we've made, racial hatred has never gone away. Only now, it has revived into new forms. Far-right nationalist movements are gathering support, seizing upon disillusionment with politics, and targeting minorities vulnerable to discrimination.

This has been most pronounced on either side of the Atlantic. In the United States, the first year of Donald Trump's presidency spawned a neo-Nazi riot in Charlottesville, Virginia, an episode made all the more troubling by Trump's praise for the 'very fine people' among the white supremacists who violently took over the streets. One year on, a militant Trump supporter in Florida mailed pipe bombs to a number of prominent liberal critics of Trump, including Barack Obama, Hillary Clinton and George Soros; and a white supremacist gunman killed eleven people and wounded six more in a Pittsburgh synagogue while yelling, 'All Jews must die'. Campaigning during the mid-term congressional elections in late 2018, Trump whipped up fears of the United States being invaded by a 'caravan' of migrants from across the southern border, and promised to end the policy of birthright citizenship enshrined in the US constitution. One Trump election advertisement was deemed so explicitly racist, no television network—not even the Trump-supporting Fox News—agreed to put it on air.

In Europe, far-right forces have gathered support in France, Germany, Italy, Sweden and elsewhere, challenging for victories in general and presidential elections; in places such as Hungary, Poland and Austria, they're already in government. In the United Kingdom, the campaign for Brexit resulted in a surge in hate crimes and in the growth of white nationalist street movements such as the English Defence League. Across Europe, Neo-Nazi and extreme nationalist parties have escaped from the fringe and are quickly establishing themselves in the mainstream.

The phenomenon is also there beyond Western democracies. The ascent of Narendra

Modi and his Bharatiya Janata Party has been accompanied by right-wing Hindu nationalism, inspiring 'cow vigilantism' and lynch mobs in many parts of rural India. In neighbouring Myanmar, ultranationalist Buddhism has fuelled anti-Muslim violence, creating the conditions for what human rights experts regard as the ethnic cleansing of the Rohingya minority. Meanwhile, in Latin America, Brazil has elected as its president Jair Bolsonaro, a politician with openly racist, sexist and homophobic views who has expressed a fondness for the country's past military dictatorship.

Australia isn't immune to this wave of intolerance. Emboldened white supremacist and anti-immigrant groups are operating in open view, having gone underground for two or three decades. But the problem goes deeper. Within our mainstream politics and media, there has been a creeping acceptance of racism and bigotry. Neo-Nazis are given sympathetic platforms on television; calls for discrimination are debated, rather than condemned as contrary to the norms of a decent society. It's got to the point where a senator can rise in parliament to call for 'the final solution to the immigration problem', as Fraser Anning did in his maiden speech in August 2018. And where the Senate, in October 2018, came perilously close to voting to endorse a motion to acknowledge 'that it is okay to be white', a slogan widely adopted by white supremacist movements.

Having spent five years in a job devoted to combating racial discrimination in Australia, it is clear to me that there has never been a more exciting time to be a dog-whistling politician or race-baiting commentator. The politics of far-right nationalism is likely only to intensify. And it will continue to challenge our values and who we are as a society. Over the decades, Australian multiculturalism has been an exemplary success. But if we're not careful, that achievement might start coming undone.

The challenge is perhaps even greater than that. Hate—specifically racial hatred—is threatening to become the new normal. If it does, it will destroy the very conditions for liberal democracy.

Whenever I think of the word hate, I imagine something connected with rage and violence.

Maybe it's because of the way we refer to hate speech, hate crimes, hate preachers, hate groups. Hate comes to us in the form of explosive hostility, stirred up by sweaty firebrands and sleazy demagogues.

But hate isn't to be detected by just the manner of its delivery. Often, in fact, it presents itself as supported by cool reason, or by appealing to positive sentiments. Misogyny can be cloaked with appeals to quasi-scientific facts about the inferiority of women. Hostility towards gays, lesbians or transgender people can be presented as an exercise of religious freedoms. Racial and religious animosity is explained away as defiance of the conformist rules of political correctness. Incitement to terrorism frequently taps into sympathisers' feelings of altruism and compassion.

Ideologies of hate often seek to appear benign or at least subject to debate, and do more damage if they succeed in doing either.

There are, you might say, many expressions of hate. It's there when people voice their dislike of a group. It's there, too, when people perform an act of discrimination. It can be on open display or come in disguise. A person can hate another but put on a front of friendship; at other times, they can struggle to contain their sense of disgust or contempt.

Hate also comes in degrees. What begins as something seemingly innocuous—a joke, an offhand remark, or some crude language—can, if left unchallenged, grow into something malicious. Words and stereotypes can grow into prejudice and discrimination. In its more serious forms, hate enters into our institutions and starts to reproduce itself through the generations. At the very apex of hate's pyramid, there is violence and genocide.

Hate isn't just one thing in essence. It's a syndrome, a group of symptoms that go together. When we hate someone, we are filled with a passionate desire to see them suffer injury, lose their power, or even be destroyed. We feel no loyalty to them, just the opposite; we would seize, even design, the opportunity to betray them. That there can be calculation in hate means it isn't a simple emotion. It isn't merely an excited feeling or reaction. It can also embody a judgment about someone's worth, and a commitment to act upon it.[2]

The multiple character of hate extends to its sources. Often, hate comes from the anger of being wronged, and not having the power to strike back. When we're helpless, resentment festers. We can brood on our lack of power and obsess about our revenge. As the nineteenth-century German philosopher Friedrich Nietzsche wrote in his account of *ressentiment*, there can be a 'sublime self-deception', which leads to the spirit of vengeance being transformed into a passion of righteousness.[3]

Another source is fear. The hate directed at a person or group can come from a fear that they pose a threat, if not to physical safety then to one's way of life. They may pose a corrupting influence on one's standards or values. Or maybe they are to be hated because they threaten one's relative position.

Given that so much of hate is about power and status, it's not surprising to find racial hatred its most salient expression today. Those dislocated by social change resent immigrants and minorities, and are anxious about their place in society. In any case, race and hate remain elemental. Ideas about race and power have been present in the foundation of many modern nations. Hate has been a regular companion, providing justifications for imperial conquests, the enslavement of peoples, and projects of colonial annihilation.

Australian society has certainly been shaped profoundly by race and hate. The arrival of the British—experienced by Aboriginal peoples as an invasion—brought to the Australian continent a particular conception of civilisation and the hierarchy of peoples, races and cultures. It was there in the British claim of sovereignty, and the assertion of the doctrine of *terra nullius*. At least sixty thousand years of Aboriginal occupation was rendered legally (and for all other practical purposes) null and void because the British didn't consider Aboriginal people to be a civilised race by white, European standards.

Some may say that it's uncharitable to ascribe racism to British colonisation, that the intentions of the British were noble and benevolent. But it's hard to deny the presence of hate in the Australian colony, right from the beginning. We can say this based on firsthand sources. Captain Watkin Tench, who arrived on the First Fleet, and penned the first detailed published account of life in Sydney, described the local Aboriginal population's reception of the colonists. 'They seemed studiously to avoid us, either from fear, jealousy or hatred', Tench wrote, explaining that 'the unprovoked outrages committed upon them, by unprincipled individuals among us, caused the evils we had experienced'.[4]

These outrages were nothing less than the acts of colonial violence dealt to Aboriginal people. In British eyes, the settlement of Australia was about taming a harsh land whose hostile natives needed to be subjugated or pacified. There was sexual violence, bloodshed, even massacres. During the 'frontier wars' between European colonial arrivals and Aboriginal locals between 1788 and the 1930s, at least thirty thousand Aboriginal people (and about two thousand Europeans) were killed.[5]

Hate was part of the destructive and creative energy of all colonisation. And it was a brutal instrument of the Australian colony's expansion and consolidation, though one frequently downplayed in historical accounts.

Consider the case of Lachlan Macquarie, regarded by many as the most significant of the colonial governors of New South Wales. His record is stained by the Appin massacre of 1816, among the more notorious of frontier massacres. A detachment of soldiers deployed by Macquarie to the south west of Sydney slaughtered and beheaded Aboriginal people of the Dharawal nation (first estimates placed it at fourteen dead, but historians believe the number to be much higher). Macquarie's instructions were for the soldiers to fire upon and compel to surrender any 'natives' they encountered who made 'the least show of resistance'. 'Such natives as happened to be killed on such occasions, if grown up men, are to be hanged up on Trees in Conspicuous Situations, to Strike the Survivors with the greater terror', Macquarie ordered. His men hanged two men and one woman in the trees, before decapitating them, the heads ending up as exhibits in the University of Edinburgh until being returned to Australia in 1991.[6]

Only in more recent years has Macquarie's record as governor been questioned. His entry in the *Australian Dictionary of Biography* is an example of the orthodox rendering of history. Macquarie is described as pursuing a policy towards the Aboriginal population which was 'an expression of the same humanitarian concerns' brought to other colonial matters. 'No other governor since Phillip', the entry continues, 'had shown them so much sympathy'.[7] It's a revealing demonstration of how history books treat Aboriginal deaths with casual disregard.

By the mid-1800s, the task of taming the frontier was largely accomplished. Yet race persisted as a civic principle, one anchored in fear. In the colonial imagination, Australia faced a physical threat from the coloured peoples of the world, especially the teeming yellow hordes in Asia. Charles Pearson, a leading liberal figure in the Victorian colony, predicted that, 'the day will come, and perhaps is not far distant, when the European observer will look round to see the globe circled with a continuous zone of the black and yellow races, no longer too weak for aggression or under tutelage, but independent'. The white races were in danger of being 'elbowed and hustled, and perhaps even thrust aside by peoples whom we looked down upon as servile and thought of as bound always to minister to our needs'.[8]

When political nationhood was achieved, in the form of federation, it would also bear a racial stamp in the form of White Australia. 'Unity of race', as declared by then attorney-general and future prime minister Alfred Deakin, 'is an absolute essential to the unity of Australia'.[9] The first substantive pieces of legislation passed by the new national parliament were the *Pacific Island Labourers Act 1901*, which expelled all Pacific Islanders working in Australia, and the *Immigration Restriction Act 1901*, which was concerned with limiting non-British immigration to Australia and with deporting undesirable aliens in Australia.

We've come a long way since then. The advocates of a White Australia would have been horrified to countenance today's society, one which reflects the successive waves of immigration following the end of World War II. Nearly half of the population is either born overseas or has a parent who was born overseas. On one estimate, about 21 per cent of Australians have a non-European background, with another 3 per cent being of Indigenous background.[10]

Even so, the imprint of race and hate remains, if not indelible then difficult to erase. The ideal of White Australia was seminal. For all the success of Australian multiculturalism, and the evolving nature of the national identity, we remain conditioned by its cultural power.

The mere mention of the words 'White Australia' is enough to conjure in our minds a certain picture of nationhood, and its related anxieties. The popular and cultural definition of who is authentically Australian remains, for the most part, a white European one. Whether it's the media and the stories we are told about the nation, or the senior leadership of just about all our major institutions, pause for a moment and you get the message that the place is still run by a particular section of society, defined by its whiteness (largely male). While almost a quarter of the Australian population has a non-European or Indigenous background, only 3 per cent of the country's chief executives have such backgrounds. In 2018, my colleagues and I found that, among the 370-odd chief executives and equivalents in Australian business, government, politics and higher education, there was barely a cricket team's worth of leaders who had a non-European background.[11]

Whiteness in Australia involves a hierarchy of belonging. It's what explains why too often, white Anglo–Celtic and European Australians feel entitled to determine who truly counts as Australian. Whiteness, thus understood, is systemic and institutional. It's not necessarily exercised with conscious knowledge. It's something that operates in the background, part of the unspoken norms and unwritten rules that guide how society operates.[12]

Racial minorities quickly assimilate an idea of whiteness, again unconsciously or without a great deal of thought. While I was growing up, my parents were quick to impress upon me that I was Australian; we had the citi-zenship certificates to prove it. But it was an insistence that betrayed an insecurity and aspiration, as opposed to an attained reality. We knew that an 'Aussie' meant a white Australian, at least that's how everyone else understood it. Throughout my teenage years, I wouldn't have necessarily described myself as Australian. It was only when I spent five years studying in England, where others would describe me as Australian, that I became used to thinking of myself that way. Back at home, I was more accustomed to being referred to as an Asian. It felt like I was an Australian everywhere but in my own country.

Whiteness matters. It shapes how we talk about issues, and who has the right to talk with authority. When it's in play, it frequently leaves racial minorities as passive players in public debates. Minorities are talked about, but infrequently seen or heard, even when the debate is about them.

When minorities do speak out, they can be made to feel that no one in power listens. Many Aboriginal and Torres Strait Islander Australians, for example, took umbrage with the Turnbull government's rejection of the Uluru Statement from the Heart in 2017. The culmination of extensive dialogues with Aboriginal and Torres Strait Islander communities, conceived by the Referendum Council on constitutional recognition, the Uluru Statement proposed a guaranteed voice for Indigenous people in the form of an advisory body to parliament. It was an eloquent blueprint for Aboriginal reconciliation. The government, though, summarily dismissed it, arguing that such a body would be seen as a 'third chamber' of parliament, which couldn't possibly win endorsement at a referendum. The result was another abortive attempt to secure constitutional recognition of First Australians. Law professor Megan Davis, one of the authors of the Uluru Statement, described it as a ruthless rejection, and a demonstration of 'the torment of our powerlessness'.[13]

The voices of minorities can be aggressively policed, as well. I've detected this whenever I've taken part in public debates about race issues. It's that old notion of Go Back to Where You Came From. Almost without fail, an opponent somewhere will resort to saying that I've somehow—as an Australian of Asian

heritage who came here as an immigrant—
displayed a lack of gratitude to the nation in
offering an opinion that may challenge something about Australian society. It's as though
the right to express one's opinion in our
democracy is meant to exist for some only in
theory. Some will always believe their claim
to being heard is superior. To be an Australian
citizen doesn't mean that others will believe
you are an equal, or believe you truly belong.
It doesn't guarantee that others will see you
as *really* Australian.

A racialised sense of nationhood doesn't
always involve hate. When people draw lines
about who is Australian and who isn't, there
can be many forces at play. It could merely
reflect a failure of imagination or a narrow-
ness of experience with racial diversity.

Indifference and ignorance can overlap with racial hatred, but aren't always themselves expressions of it.

Whiteness becomes an active hatred, however, when it's channelled as anger. When anger is directed at people like Adam Goodes or Yassmin Abdel-Magied—people turned into figures of hate—it's because some find it intolerable for an Aboriginal Australian or a person of colour to question aspects of the national identity. Hate is when an opinionated member of a minority comes to be regarded as an uppity ingrate who doesn't know their place.

Fear is the other emotion that activates whiteness into hatred. Haters may fear they are losing the power to define the boundaries of the national identity. They may be anxious that the hierarchy of voice within Australian society is under challenge, that there is a decline in the authority of Anglo-Celtic or European Australia.

When people are moved to racial hatred, it transforms the way they see others. Hate crimes against a certain group can be committed by people who may have had no history of animosity towards the group. It's not unheard of for people to turn against their own colleagues and neighbours. In the most extreme instances, as in the Rwandan genocide of the 1990s, previously close friends end up committing murderous violence upon each other.

The effects can be more insidious. Once it's released into the ether, hate poisons trust. When Pauline Hanson infamously declared in 1996 that Australia was being 'swamped by Asians', this amounted to a direct assault on people like me and my family. The damage, though, wasn't confined to how Hanson's language invited others to label us 'gooks' or 'slopes'. The feeling of exclusion and humiliation didn't have to come from outright abuse. Others may have refrained from racist epithets or heated rhetoric, but when they said, 'Pauline has a point', the effect was the same, if not more troubling. When I heard a line like that from family friends or teachers, it made me think twice about where they stood. It planted doubt where there wasn't any before.

The effects of hate are turned inwards, as well as out. The targets of racialised hate can absorb it and convert it into self-hatred. Those who experience racism often take on the stereotypes directed at them, convinced of their own supposed deficiency or perversity.

Internalised racism is at play when migrant children wince when their parents speak to them in public in their native tongue. When the brown-skinned child covets the fair-skinned doll, because they know their friends think the brown-skinned doll is ugly. When the Asian teenager wants different shaped eyes, thinking they couldn't otherwise be considered beautiful or desirable. This is how racism—to be precise, the idea of whiteness—colonises the consciousness. It dominates by getting under one's skin, and into one's minds.

It doesn't always happen as a result of a particular person's design. Again, we may not even be aware of it happening. As a child, I was taught early about my family's origins and heritage. I understood that my parents were born in Laos, and that my father's family was

Chinese and my mother's was Lao. But my ideas about what was normal came as much from what was around us in society as from my parents at home, no matter what they may have said. It was rare to see on television or in popular culture anything other than a white face, certainly very few faces resembled those of my family and relatives. When I watched a John Wayne Western, I was cheering for him and the cowboys, not the Indians. Reading stories about Captain Cook, I identified with him and the British, not the 'natives' he encountered. As a child, when I looked into a mirror I may have been seeing a distorted image.

There is cunning in racism. It's programmed to operate on autopilot. When it is deliberately perpetrated, it can also be done with a high level of sophistication. People know they can't be caught out being openly racist. Hate gets disguised as humour or clumsiness, or with just enough room left for plausible deniability. In the hands of a skillful practitioner, it is deftly delivered with impeccable respectability.

The physical side of racism still exists, of course. To be exposed to racial hatred is to experience something visceral. And if it happens enough times, it can cause prolonged, even permanent harm. I've heard many Aboriginal advocates and leaders speak about how racism hurts and kills their people, a point that isn't merely made figuratively. Racism has well documented effects on its targets' health. It creates stresses and feeds disorders. Its trauma is rarely fleeting.

But the psychology behind racial hatred remains the same. When hate gets physical, it's the brutal expression of those at the top of the hierarchy who believe others are objects, subject to their will. And for those who experience it, it's a reminder that there are some in society who believe they are endowed with the authority to deal with you as they see fit. This is the message sent by a public demonstration of bigotry: don't forget there are some prepared to deal this out to you, don't forget to know your station.

We often regard such eruptions of violence as the archetype of racial hatred. Yet the more I've seen of racism, the more ambivalent I've become about seeing it that way. The potency of hate may reside as much in its banality, as in its shock value. Sometimes hate can be

It began in January 2018 with a panic about 'African gangs' in Melbourne. According to Home Affairs Minister Peter Dutton, Victorians were 'scared to go out to restaurants' because of 'African gang violence'. In the months that followed, then prime minister Malcolm Turnbull joined in to declare there was 'real concern' about Sudanese gangs. The Victorian Liberal opposition focused relentlessly on race and crime in its campaigning for November's state election (a campaign that Victorian voters emphatically rejected when they delivered the Labor government a landslide re-election).[14]

Debates about multiculturalism and immigration, more broadly speaking, have returned. In July 2018, the Minister for Citizenship and Multicultural Affairs Alan Tudge warned that

Australia was veering towards a 'European separatist multicultural model'. Along with his foray into the African gangs issue, Dutton proposed that white South African farmers deserve 'special attention' for fast-tracked humanitarian visas because of their alleged persecution on the grounds of race. Former prime minister Tony Abbott questioned whether Australia should accept any migrants at all from Africa, suggesting they are 'difficult to integrate'.[15]

There was a brief moment when it appeared the march of racism was met and turned around. Fraser Anning's 'final solution' speech in the Senate was rejected by nearly the entire parliament in August 2018. It was a false dawn. Just two months later, the Senate flirted with endorsing Pauline Hanson's motion to acknowledge 'the deplorable rise of anti-white racism and attacks on Western Civilisation' and 'that it is okay to be white'. The motion was only narrowly defeated, thirty-one votes to twenty-eight, with twenty-three government senators voting in support of Hanson. Numerous government figures even declared their vote as a principled statement of anti-racism. Attorney-General Christian Porter tweeted that, 'The Government Senators' actions in the Senate this afternoon confirm that the Government deplores racism of any kind'. Only when there was public outcry did the government retreat from its vote and declare that it had been one big 'administrative error' (apparently the result of a misunderstanding by a staff member of the Attorney-General's office).[16]

The mainstreaming of hate isn't confined to Canberra. It's happening at the grassroots of political parties. In October 2018, the ABC reported on a covert plot by some far-right groups to join major political parties, with the aim of influencing their policy agendas from within. There is evidence that the New South Wales Nationals Party had been infiltrated by members of The New Guard group, whose numbers include many self-described fascists and avowed anti-Semites.[17]

The return of race politics hasn't happened in a vacuum. In the background, sections of the media have agitated for an end to the policy of multiculturalism and have derided a non-discriminatory immigration policy. Prominent right-wing commentator Andrew Bolt has led the way, arguing there is 'a tidal wave of immigrants' overwhelming the country. Jews, Indians and Chinese are forming ethnic 'colonies' across the country, according to Bolt, 'turning this country from a home into a hotel'. Bolt has called on people to 'resist this colonising of Australia while there is still an "us" who can'.[18]

More generally, parts of the conservative media have sharpened their approach to race. The Sky News television channel appears to be emulating Fox News in the United States, becoming a network tilted towards aggressive right-wing political commentary. It has provided a sympathetic forum for visiting North American commentators associated with the alt-right, such as Milo Yiannopoulos and Lauren Southern. In a much-criticised move, one of its hosts, Adam Giles, conducted a soft interview with far-right agitator and convicted criminal Blair Cottrell. This is the same Cottrell who has called for every classroom in Australia to be adorned with a portrait of Adolf Hitler, and who has been convicted of breaching the *Victorian Racial and Religious Tolerance Act 2001*.

Other Sky News hosts, such as Rowan Dean and Ross Cameron, regularly inflame racial sentiment. In one example in 2017, following some comments I made about the lack of cultural diversity in Australian media, Dean drew attention on air to my Lao heritage, and called for me to 'hop on a plane and go back to Laos'.[19] Dean escaped any sanction from Sky News, though his co-host Cameron wasn't so lucky in November 2018, when he was sacked over comments referring to 'black-haired, slanty-eyed, yellow-skinned Chinese'.[20]

It's not just Sky News that is accommo-dating more divisive commentary. Channel Seven has run news stories featuring Cottrell, describing him and his supporters as a 'neighbourhood watch' group seeking to help 'average Australians' deal with 'an immi-grant crime crisis'.[21] In the lead-up to the 2016 election, the network retained Pauline Hanson as a paid contributor, featuring her prominently on its *Sunrise* program. Even the ABC has flirted with hate. When *Four Corners* anchor Sarah Ferguson conducted a one-on-one interview with former Trump adviser and far-right figurehead Steve Bannon, she declared in the interview there was 'no evi-dence' Bannon was a racist (notwithstanding his history of facilitating advocacy of a white ethno-state through the *Breitbart* news website, of which he was executive chairman).

Then there's the rest of News Corp. The Murdoch group's newspapers—in particular, *The Australian*, the *Daily Telegraph* and the *Herald Sun*—have ramped up their coverage of issues linked to the culture wars. Focused on imagined existential threats to Western civilisation, the so-called virtue signalling of leftist political correctness, and the alleged reverse racist agenda of human rights bodies, such coverage is aimed at fomenting nationalist rage. The hate isn't restricted to race issues, it must be said. The coverage of issues such as climate change, energy and same-sex marriage follows a similar pattern of generating hyper-partisan anger, directed at an elitist left. It's a media style defined by combative identity politics, which turns just about every issue into a culture wars contest over values.

These developments are part of the monetisation of hate. Sections of a fracturing media industry, under strain from technological transformation, seem to be using hate as part of their business model. Faced with competition from a proliferation of news and entertainment sources, some media outlets are using racial controversies to grab attention, generate clicks, and cling onto their audiences. Race-baiting has become an instrument of commercial viability.

One thing needs to be made clear: it'd be too neat to think that race politics simply reflects media commentary. If anything, the new permissibility of racism can be traced back to the government of Tony Abbott in 2013. As I'll explain shortly, the Abbott government's unsuccessful push to repeal section 18C of the Racial Discrimination Act signalled to a certain faction of society that they were now at liberty to vent racial hostility and claim the protection of free speech. Then there was the double dissolution election called by Malcolm Turnbull in 2016. By returning Hanson and three One Nation senators to Canberra, that election guaranteed the far-right a foothold in the parliament.

It's not just that mainstream politicians on the centre-right of Australian politics have failed to deal effectively with far-right populism; they've contributed to its rise. In the months leading up to the 2016 election, then prime minister Malcolm Turnbull made it plain that he believed Hanson 'is not a welcome presence on the Australian political scene'. Yet the Turnbull government adopted a conciliatory tone towards Hanson after the election, effectively normalising her presence in national politics. The Liberal Party even put One Nation ahead of its Coalition partners, the Nationals, in the West Australian state election of 2017. Turnbull's lieutenant, Senator Arthur Sinodinos, defended the move by declaring that Pauline Hanson and One Nation were now 'a lot more sophisticated' and 'a very different beast' to what they were in the 1990s.[23]

The figures of mainstream politics were themselves beginning to turn sharply to the right. In February 2018, newly appointed New South Wales Liberal senator Jim Molan was found to have posted two racist propaganda videos produced by Britain First, a far-right group in the United Kingdom. In 2017, Molan (then a retired army general) called for the mass internment of Muslims and terror suspects without trial, proposing that candidates for internment be put before a new tribunal consisting of a judge and 'non-jurist' members. As journalist Jacqueline Maley observed, 'the far-right movement could not ask for a better or more respectable front than the office of a Liberal senator with an honourable record of military service'.[24]

What is happening here can't be divorced from the global shifts occurring on the political right. The Trump presidency in the United States has animated hardline conservative and far-right forces. By flouting old rules, Trumpian nationalism has redefined

Western political debates. It has shown how conservative politics can be energised when an effective demagogue comes along and liberates their followers from the strictures of civility. It has transformed centre-right politics in many countries into a force of reactionary, nativist populism. Trump may not have succeeded in making America great again, but he has made white tribalism great again around the world.

Understanding Trump's rise requires appreciating the organised forces behind his politics. Trump's success has been synonymous with, and enabled by, the emergence of the so-called alt-right. Described by many as a movement or a political bloc, the alt-right brings together several different extremist groupings: racial supremacists and neo–Nazis seeking a white ethno-state; neo-reactionaries who wish to see democracy replaced by autocracy; libertarian anarchists and 'shitposters' who revel in anonymously trolling the internet; and members of the 'manosphere' who identify with misogynist ideology. Making its original mark within online comment boards such as 4chan and reddit, and through the 'Gamergate' controversy within the video games subculture, the alt-right came to find its political voice through outlets such as *Breitbart*.[25]

The alt-right is a strange collection of players, but one united by a preoccupation with the culture wars. Its followers seek to replace the right-wing conservative establishment, which it regards as effetely ceding the west to non-white elements. One tendency of the alt-right—the 'alt-light', associated with internet personalities such as Milo Yiannopoulos and Gavin McInnes—has come to assume particular influence. Defined by a transgressive and youthful style, ostensibly aimed at skewering political correctness, the 'alt-light' has been a bridge between the old-fashioned white supremacist extremism of neo-Nazi political organisations and mainstream Republican Trumpism.[26] Through digital memes, humour, propaganda, conspiracy theories and other media interventions, the tendency aims to shift the 'Overton window' that defines the range of policies the public will regard as acceptable—to make ideas about 'white genocide' and the establishment of a white ethno-state, for example, palatable enough to become part of mainstream debates.

The success of the alt-right style has been replicated here in Australia. It's reflected in stunts such as those delivered by Hanson and Anning in parliament. Moreover, as in the United States, our mainstream media has been slow to grasp the true nature of far-right politics. Far-right extremists are routinely described as 'right-wing provocateurs', as though advocacy of racism and violence were forgivable maverick excesses. But when we accept such characterisations, we give these extremists exactly what they're after: the veneer of respectability, maybe even the appearance of exciting novelty. We sanitise their politics and we validate their presence. The political culture shifts to accommodate them. Perhaps we need to call the alt-right for what it is: the wolf of white supremacism dressed up in hipster clothing.

Australia may be especially vulnerable to a white supremacist style of political subversion. It's because we have a tendency to be so sensitive about charges of racism. Many people refer to racism through euphemisms, so as to ease white discomfort. Something is 'racially charged' or 'racially insensitive'— but only in extreme cases is something ever 'racist'. When something does warrant such a description, people draw distinctions between *doing* something that is racist and *being* a racist, or between having an *intention* to commit a racist act and merely doing something that has an *effect* described as racist. Never mind that racism is as much about the effect as it is about the intention; never mind that being racist usually means, well, doing something racist.

The evasion, though, follows a pattern. Any claim about racism is fiercely contested. People resist making any concession that it exists, because it would mean that Australia is an irredeemably racist nation. Often it seems that the real offence isn't to do something racist, but to call someone racist for having done it. This is perfect soil for far-right propaganda to take root. Caught up in the national habit of denying that something is truly or really racist, people end up missing the racism happening before their eyes.

As for the consequences, the damage of hate is, as I've said, physical as well as psychological. And significant though it is, the damage goes beyond just what its targets endure directly. When hate creates fear and intimidation, there is also a chilling effect. If you've copped such treatment, you'll think twice about standing up to something, or about speaking out. Our democracy ends up losing voices it would otherwise hear in that supposed marketplace of ideas. Citizens suffer the indignity of living in a democracy but feeling second-rate.

Anger and fear also cut both ways. Those who know hate can come to know it too well, and learn to return the hate. In *The Fire Next Time*, James Baldwin wrote of his experience as a black American in mid-twentieth-century New York. In order to be free as a black man, he wrote, one needed more than a bank account, 'one needed a handle, a lever, a means of inspiring fear'. When it came to how white Americans treated blacks, 'neither civilised reason nor Christian love would cause any of those people to treat you as they presumably wanted to be treated; only the fear of your power to retaliate would cause them to do that'.[27]

So how are we to deal with hate? How are we to counter a race politics built on anger and fear?

An obvious place to start is leadership. We must expect and demand that political leaders defend us from the dangers of hate, rather than expose us to them. They must understand that any partisan advantage to be gained from stoking resentment is overwhelmed by the damage it does to the harmony and stability of society.

I suspect many of the politicians who conduct race politics don't do it out of a doctrinal commitment to racial purity (with some obvious exceptions). Many likely do so out of cynicism, and with a misplaced confidence that they can repair any harm done. The arrogance of politics, in every age, is to believe that parliaments and governments have the power to control the forces they unleash; that they will be the masters of social forces, as opposed to their slaves. It's just that the liberation of racial sentiment can cause more than just a minor fraying of the social fabric.

Many would say that today's descent into race politics was presaged years earlier. In 1996, Hanson's maiden speech in parliament failed to attract a strong condemnation from then prime minister John Howard. Howard's response was to defend her right to free speech, and to affirm that the 'pall of censorship on certain issues' had been lifted.[28] The effect on race relations was invidious. It created a new political climate in which those who used their free speech to criticise racism became upended into the enemies of free speech themselves.

There are also the refugee policies that have been progressively adopted since the introduction of mandatory detention of asylum seekers in 1992. The acceptance of mandatory detention as a deterrent against the arrival of asylum seekers by boat has inured the Australian electorate to the necessity of tough love. It opened the door to the cruelty of indefinite offshore detention of asylum seekers in Nauru and

Manus Island. While Australia's hardline refugee policies haven't involved racial discrimination in a formal sense—there hasn't been any direct discrimination based on racial or ethnic backgrounds—their effects have implicated race in de facto form. Overwhelmingly, it's brown-skinned people from the Middle East and Asia who are in refugee detention centres, and who are associated with being 'illegal immigrants'.

It's significant that they're also predominantly Muslim. The fusion of refugee issues, border security and terrorism has proven to be a powerful one for politicians. Since the September 11 attacks in 2001, anxieties about national security have fuelled anti-Muslim hatred. It's made the proposition for a hardliner on national security a simple one:

namely, that we must keep the borders strong against asylum seekers and to detain them off-shore, because we would otherwise let in some people who are likely terrorist threats.

When terror incidents do occur, political leaders can be quick to escalate their calls for Muslim communities to do more. Instead of cautioning against judging entire communities against the extremism of a few, they make political mileage out of tough rhetoric against Muslims. Prime Minister Scott Morrison did this in November 2018, when he made vehement criticisms of Muslims for not stopping extremism, following the terror incident in Melbourne's Bourke Street. Others seem to go especially out of their way to insult and goad Muslims, as Hanson did in August 2017 when she entered the Senate chamber wearing a burqa, theatrically casting it off before making a speech.

It needn't be this way, of course. Political leaders ultimately do have the power to shape society. They mightn't always be able to control social forces for their own ends, but they do set the tone for the nation. When politicians model civility and restraint, they help to temper people's passions. And when they employ red-hot rhetoric, or target particular communities, that can help set things aflame.

Hateful speech can spur others to take hateful action. The obvious example is that of the United States, where the recent increase in far-right political violence and terror there seems hard to divorce from the vitriolic statements of Trump as president.

The suggestion here isn't that Trump has directly called for specific acts of far-right violence and terror. Rather, it's that the encouragement by Trump for his supporters to take matters into their own hands lends political legitimacy to the desire some may feel to express their violent tendencies. This is what some have called 'stochastic terrorism', or the use of political communication 'to incite random actors to carry out violent or terrorist acts that are statistically predictable but individually unpredictable'.[29] If you whip up an atmosphere of hatred, and give people permission to act upon their hatred, don't be surprised to find someone, somewhere taking up the invitation. It's a point we seem to understand better in contexts other than race. When we talk about Islamic hate preachers, for example, few would hesitate to agree their speech can encourage division and inspire violence.

Australia has been fortunate not to have its politics captured by as talented a demagogue as Trump. Even so, some of our politicians have given licence to racial hatred. They've done so in a systematic fashion, targeting the legal foundation of our racial equality and multiculturalism. On two occasions, in 2014 and 2017, the Coalition government moved to amend the Racial Discrimination Act, cheered on by prominent sections of the media and the right-wing Institute of Public Affairs think tank.

The cause of repealing section 18C of the Act—which makes it unlawful to do an act that is reasonably likely to offend, insult, humiliate or intimidate someone on the grounds of their race—has been totemic for the right. Section 18C grew in public prominence following the federal court case in 2011, which found *Herald Sun* columnist Andrew Bolt to have breached section 18C because of a series of articles he had written about fair-skinned Aboriginal people. In more recent years, a case pursued under section 18C against students at the Queensland University of Technology (eventually dismissed in a federal court), and a complaint made against cartoonist Bill Leak (which was shortly after withdrawn by the complainant), have given conservatives and libertarians rallying points for their campaign.

On both occasions, the push for legislative amendment failed. The Abbott government in August 2014 abandoned its attempt to repeal section 18C in the face of significant public opposition, and following a widespread backlash to George Brandis's suggestion that 'people have a right to be bigots'.[30] In March 2017, the Turnbull government's bill to amend section 18C was defeated in a vote on the Senate floor. But while the Act remains intact, a good deal of damage was done. When you have the Attorney-General of Australia defending a right to bigotry on the floor of parliament, when you make the cause of free speech synonymous with a desire to inflict racial vilification on others, it changes the political climate.

What happened with the Racial Discrimination Act was a case study of failed political leadership. It's what can happen when policy is dictated by ideological zeal. You end up not only with a government taken wildly off course, but also with a warped political debate. The rhetoric attached to changing section 18C epitomises culture wars hysteria. According to its critics, the Racial Discrimination Act is political correctness gone mad—a flawed expression of 'cultural Marxism' and multicultural identity politics. It stifles public debates because people fear that speaking frankly will lead them to be branded racist by progressives intent on 'virtue-signalling'. Perhaps most grievously, the Act represents how ethnic and racial minorities are afforded greater protections under anti-discrimination law than members of 'mainstream Australia', who suffer the real discrimination in the form of reverse racism.

Let's consider this idea that political correctness has shut down debates about race. It's hard to see how debates have been shut down when *The Australian* has devoted hundreds of thousands of words to attacking the Racial Discrimination Act. When there are regular racialised campaigns on crime, immigration and Australian history in the *Herald Sun* and the *Daily Telegraph*. When nocturnal panels on Sky News endlessly berate multiculturalism and denigrate minorities. When Pauline Hanson makes regular appearances on *Sunrise* and *Today* to give us a breakfast serving of her warped politics. From broadsheets to tabloids, from morning to night-time viewing on television, and from the backbench to the dispatch box in parliament, there's plenty of race-baiting happening.

As for identity politics, much of the debate about the Racial Discrimination Act and free speech is indeed about identity politics. But it's a white identity politics aimed at reinforcing a hierarchy of voice and power in Australian society. Complaints about the Act suffocating free speech are, in large part, about a resentment of minorities being able to speak back through the law. They're the complaints of those who can't hack it when others challenge their racism.

It goes without saying it's vital our society maintains legal protections against racial hatred. This is because laws set the standard in our society. Over time, such standards will shape attitudes and regulate conduct. Even if such laws mightn't always succeed in deterring or reforming the more extreme elements intent on hate speech, they still help to broadcast what's acceptable and what isn't to the rest of society. They keep us from conceding ground to the fringe.

The vast majority of Australians agree it's important to legislate against racial hatred. For example, in March 2017, a Fairfax-Ipsos poll found that 78 per cent of people believed it should remain unlawful to offend, insult or humiliate people on the basis of their race or ethnicity. A similarly high number (about 85 per cent) support multiculturalism, according to regular surveys of public opinion.[31]

There is wide acceptance that, in a multicultural Australia, any freedom of expression shouldn't come at the expense of a freedom from discrimination; one person's freedom doesn't extend to taking away another's freedom. There is already strong protection of free speech, including in the Racial Discrimination Act itself. When I've explained to people that the Act in fact protects free speech under the provision of section 18D—which ensures that any public discussion or comment is exempted from section 18C, provided it is done reasonably and in good faith—there is often genuine bafflement about why the legislation has been so contentious.

There are admittedly limits to what legislation can achieve. I'm not saying that you can legislate away racial hatred with the stroke of a pen. Laws on their own don't eradicate social ills. Section 18C won't cure prejudice, even though it attaches public opprobrium to racial hatred. But think of it this way: for as long as there has been civilisation, there have been laws against murder and theft. The fact that murder and theft still occur doesn't lead us to conclude we should abandon laws against the crimes.

Clearly, hate demands a social response, in addition to legislation. There is a particular need in Australia for one kind of social transformation: a new ability to talk about racism without defensiveness or apprehension. We have a national aversion to speaking directly about racism. Around the world, on 21 March every year, nations mark the International Day for the Elimination of Racial Discrimination, a day promulgated by the United Nations. Here, we know it instead as Harmony Day. The rebadging occurred during the 1990s, the result of the Howard government's desire to create a more positive-sounding day. In a similar vein, during 2018, Attorney-General Christian Porter floated the idea of renaming the office of Race Discrimination Commissioner to something such as the Community Relations Commissioner or Community Harmony Commissioner. According to Porter, the role should not be 'divisive' or 'contribute to division'.[32]

Listen to the likes of Porter, and you get the impression that anti-racism is the real source of social division, and not racism itself. That the best response to racism is not to confront it, but to focus on the positives. This is a take on race that I came to know pretty well. While I was Race Discrimination Commissioner, I was accustomed to seeing columns in News Corp newspapers or panels on Sky News criticising me for allegedly fomenting social division, or for creating a problem out of racial discrimination when one didn't apparently exist.

Pause for a moment, and consider all this. How can we fight racism, if we aren't even able to name it? How, exactly, does racism get diminished with the power of positive thinking?

Those who fight hate get told all the time to tread more gently. In his 'Letter from a Birmingham Jail', Martin Luther King Jr wrote of his conclusion that the greatest obstacle to racial justice in the United States was not the extremists of the Ku Klux Klan but rather the 'white moderate'. This is the moderate 'who is more devoted to "order" than to justice; who prefers a negative peace which is the absence of tension to a positive peace which is the presence of justice'. As King wrote, 'shallow understanding from people of goodwill is more frustrating than absolute understanding from people of ill will. Lukewarm acceptance is much more bewildering than outright rejection'.[33]

In my time as an anti-racism advocate, few things have been as exasperating as this. So much energy is spent on the denial and deflection of racism's existence. Imagine if that energy were spent instead on fighting prejudice and discrimination. Imagine if there weren't such a hang up about being called out for questionable conduct. We'd be in a better place if people were prepared to accept that if you don't wish to be called racist or bigoted, you can simply avoid acting in a racist or bigoted way in the first place.

If we're serious about combatting racial hatred, we need to be more literate about matters of race. All too often, people default to declarations about their colour-blindness: 'I don't see race or colour.' I can understand why this is done. It's hard to question your way of seeing the world. It's disorienting to focus your mind on the things society has rendered invisible. To do so can expose 'white fragility', the defensiveness that white people exhibit when their ideas about race are challenged, and when they feel implicated in ideas of white supremacy.[34] However, progress on race will be impossible if people can't vanquish this fragility.

Fighting hate also requires us to accept that good intentions aren't enough. If they're accompanied by a misdiagnosis of the problem, then they end up meaning very little.

Those on the political left can be as culpable as those on the right. There are well-meaning liberals and progressives, for example, who share the conservative view that multicultural identity politics is the cause of white racial resentment. The implication is that demands for equality and justice by minorities should be delayed, or even rolled back, in order to appease the resentful. Taking this view amounts to a deflection of responsibility. It says, in effect, that the task of countering hate falls to those who are exposed to it. It also suggests there's a moral equivalence between multiculturalists who seek a more inclusive democracy and white nationalists who wish to exclude some racial groups from the democratic community. The unspoken premise is that minorities may, yet again, need to learn their place, lest they ruin it for everyone.

We must resist such thinking. All decent people bear a responsibility to reject a race politics fuelled by hate. It's the idea of the standard you accept being the standard you're prepared to walk by. When racism occurs, it's an assault not only on our fellow citizens, but also on our values and on our freedom. We reject racism because it diminishes all of us, and because it diminishes our country.

To stand against hate and racism is, then, a patriotic responsibility. By this, I mean a patriotism very different to the aggressive national pride or popular jingoism associated with the word. A true patriotism is about the desire to see your country live up to its very best, and the readiness to work with your fellow citizens to improve it. To accept that responsibility is to believe that there is still a purpose larger than just our own self. That there is such a thing as a common good, or a public interest, that is worth defending from the debasement of hatred.

There's another common pitfall: a confusion of racial resentment with class disadvantage. This has its roots in the widely accepted idea that racism comes not from hatred, but from ignorance or some other kind of suffering. It fits with the picture we often see of racism in media. I'm referring to the typical outburst of bigotry on a bus or train, perpetrated by someone whose rage at their own condition leads them to lash out. Racism gets presented as an affliction of the downtrod-den. Bigotry becomes defined as proletarian resentment.

This ties in with the conventional wisdom about populism. A populist politics built on opposition to immigration, and appealing to wounded national pride, is on the rise, we're told, because it speaks directly to members of the working class disillusioned by main-stream elites. In the United States, Trump was elected to the White House because he was the candidate of the anxious and dispos-sessed white working class; his presidency is the product of a backlash against Democratic contempt for blue-collar workers. The vote in favour of Brexit succeeded, not because a majority in London supported it, but because large swathes of working-class regional

England had had enough of the metropolitan embrace of immigration and the European Union. In Australia, some argue that lower class white Australians are angry at middle class progressive politics because grievances about racism 'drown out lower class pain'.[35]

Race politics is rarely just about race, to be sure. It can be hard to separate the economic from the cultural and racial. Having said that, the evidence for the class thesis is far from convincing. In the United States, those who voted for Trump at the 2016 election generally had a higher mean household income than those who didn't. The strongest supporters of Trump weren't defined so much by class, as by race. As American author Ta-Nehisi Coates has written, Trump is 'the first white president' for whom 'whiteness is neither notional nor symbolic but is the very core of his power'.[36] In Australia, if we take One Nation's electoral comeback as a fair proxy, the evidence from the Australian Election Survey shows that 98 per cent of One Nation voters are Australian-born (compared with 74 per cent of the general population).[37] As with Trump and US voters, the most obvious factor isn't class, it's something else.

That there can be such misdiagnosis seems odd. But it's understandable. The politics of multiculturalism has long contained a tension between recognition and redistribution. For those on the left, the recognition of cultural identities has always been regarded as something that competes with the redistribution of income, wealth and power.

The problem may be more than just partisan in nature. It may say something about the enduring and unspeakable power of whiteness. Sometimes, even when confronted directly with racism, those who have never known the experience of bigotry struggle to make sense of it. Their vocabulary may not include race. They have to assimilate race into another category. It's why countering hate must begin with being able to see it and name it.

'Kill ugliness with kindness.' It's advice I've received many times, and put into action many times as well. Sometimes it works. If you're able to defuse hostility with some generosity, it seems worth the price. Even if one conversation doesn't do the trick, it at least sets things up for another conversation, and another. You've got to be prepared to work before you win over your adversary; you can't just pound them into submission.

Our conventional answer to hate reflects a liberal belief in goodwill and justice. The liberal instinct is to take the high road, to appeal to the better angels of our nature, to say that love and hope can conquer hate. As Michelle Obama famously said of the animosity directed at her and her husband when he was in the White House: 'When they go low, we go high.' You should let your values do the talking, and have the courage to set the better example. The other Obama said it with the words of Martin Luther King Jr: 'the arc of the moral universe is long, but it bends toward justice.'

To counter hate is to play a long game. It concerns a problem with which all liberal democracies must contend. To be a modern democrat is to accept pluralism, and the disagreement that comes with it. It's to accept that no one can ever definitively speak for 'the people', and that power must never be concentrated in one authoritative source. As societies grow more diverse—in race, ethnicity, as well as values and identities— this ability to live amid differences grows more urgent.

I've focused primarily on racial hatred, but there's a general point to be made. For a pluralist democracy to work, we must all possess a measure of civility and tolerance. To be a citizen is, in part, to show the right manners to our fellow members of society. It's to put up with views and people we don't like or agree with, it's to accept that everyone is owed a certain respect and equality, it's to keep an open mind and give others a fair hearing.

This isn't just a political vision, but a moral one. If you believe in this, you don't just think that someone is a better citizen when they act this way. You also think that acting this way makes them a better person or human being. In case it isn't clear, I believe in this conception of liberal citizenship. I believe it ultimately deserves our commitment.

But often, this liberal conception takes a twist. It takes on an absolutist interpretation, one about avoiding the taint of conflict and resisting at all times the seduction of emotions. Liberal reason must prevail, to the point that adopting a temporary posture of combat is regarded as enough to corrupt. The mere bluff of hating against hate is even, perhaps, too much. It goes to the idea once put by novelist Kurt Vonnegut: 'We are what we pretend to be, so we must be careful about what we pretend to be.'

This script is a familiar one. When Hanson was returned to parliament in 2016, for instance, some progressive voices urged us to listen rather than attack her and her followers. Any elitist sneering at racism was unfair to Hanson, who was actually 'a nice person'. Instead, we should 'welcome Hanson to the parliament' and have the conversation with her and her voters. We needed to bridge the tribal gulf opening up in our society.[38]

Is this really how we are to deal with intolerance? Is it enough to have a forgiving smile and to extend the hand of friendship?

Don't get me wrong. In order to fight hate, we must have some goodwill, enough to make sure we don't dismiss our opponents. We should seek to show them the errors of their ways. We may question someone, and respectfully take them to task, but we must leave open the possibility that they may change, and embrace them if they do. We can make peace with enemies, and take them as our friends. This was the example of civic friendship set by the Gandhis, Kings and Mandelas of the world.

When kindness overcomes hate, it's uplifting and inspiring. Since I first learned of it some years ago, I've marvelled at the story of Daryl Davis. An African-American blues musician, Davis has over the past thirty years befriended members of the Ku Klux Klan. Through gentle and patient persuasion, he has influenced more than two hundred Klansmen to leave the group. Today, Davis has a prized collection of white hooded Klan robes, which his reformed friends have given to him as thanks.[39]

But a story like this is the exception rather than the rule. Changing minds is tough, especially when humility is in short supply. Few of us are big enough to admit we're wrong when confronted with our errors. As in the case of Davis and his KKK defectors, the results can be years in the making. We'd be naïve to think that hate can be conquered through a willed surrender to love and kindness. Not least, it would result in shifting the burden of fighting hate to those who experience it the most. It seems perverse to expect that those who endure racial hatred must act like saints, and befriend their oppressors and tormentors.

I say this as a sympathetic critic, but it's a feature of progressive generosity that it conducts self-defeating gestures. There must be some limits to civility and tolerance. Some lines can't be crossed. You can't be tolerant of intolerance. You can't welcome those who seek the destruction of a liberal order. If lambs are to dine with wolves, they must know they can end up on the menu.

We need a clear understanding of the very nature of hatred. Hate isn't just about emotional hostility or irrational outbursts,

which can be remedied with rational discussion or loving care. It's ultimately about
power and dominance. Those most vulnerable to a politics of hate—and this is true not
only of the racial kind, but also other forms
of hatred—are often caught up in a system
or institutional pattern of oppression and
injustice. If this is what we're talking about,
it's guileless to believe you can just convince
those who enjoy power and dominance to
relinquish their status.

There's a second flaw of the liberal sensi-
bility, which runs in tandem with the idea of
'killing ugliness with kindness'. It concerns
the liberal ideal of reason and progress. This
says that the citizen of conviction shouldn't
be afraid of bad ideas or bad speech, but
respond to it with good ideas and good

speech. Debate drives nastiness out from underground and into open scrutiny. Once bad ideas are exposed to the disinfectant of sunlight, reason will prevail and progress can take its historic course. This is how the marketplace of ideas is meant to work.

The problem isn't about countering hate through public debate. That is, of course, something we should do. It's just that we shouldn't rely on this, and this alone. We must understand that the marketplace of ideas favours, without fail, the powerful and the privileged. Minorities and those less powerful aren't able to compete on fair terms. Not everyone in the marketplace operates by the same rules.

When it concerns free speech, our public debate frequently exhibits double standards.

Those who defend an absolutist approach to free speech can often be the first to discredit those who express views with which they disagree. Take columnist Janet Albrechtsen, a prominent critic of section 18C of the Racial Discrimination Act. According to Albrechtsen, anti-racism activists who speak out on social media are an 'online Stasi for the 21st century', who 'trawl sections of the media to clobber views they hate'.[40] To label anti-racists as Stasi, likening them to the secret police force of a communist totalitarian state, involves more than mere disagreement. It involves denying the very propriety of voicing anti-racism. With debate like this, it's only right to be sceptical about leaving everything to a competitive marketplace of ideas. You can't have blind faith in such a thing, when the self-styled champions of free speech readily demonise people who dare exercise their free speech to criticise racism and bigotry.

Even if you end up with some progress through debate, grave damage can be done in the process. Debates give ideas publicity and possibly lend them credibility. A case in point is the marriage equality debate, and the postal survey taken in 2017, which many in the LGBTI community saw as permitting homophobic and transphobic hatred to be expressed during the period of campaigning. For racial minorities, the mainstream media's accommodation of far-right voices has led to white supremacism getting a relatively free run. The so-called debate has led to the legitimation of extreme ideas.

A politics of hate must not be misdiagnosed as merely involving offensive ideas, which democracies must as a rule admit into public debate. If that were so, we must insist on the liberal necessity of giving equal time to extremism when it involves, say, paedophiles or Islamist terrorists or anti-vaccination campaigners. We seem comfortable in such instances to declare that we have to be intolerant of abhorrent views, because giving them an airing would pose a social danger. White supremacism is somehow an exception.

The ideas associated with such politics are far from democratic. They are, in fact, aimed at destroying democracy or the conditions of democratic citizenship. The writer Aleksandar Hemon highlights the gulf of understanding that exists between those who have the luxury to exchange ideas with extremists from a safe distance, and those who are directly threatened by the extremism they seek to enact. What is for some privileged liberals 'a matter of a potentially productive difference in opinion' is for those targeted by racism 'a matter of basic survival'. As Hemon explains, some ideas 'are inflicted upon people of colour and immigrants, who do not experience them as ideas but as violence'.[41]

It's a gulf I've seen many times. I've heard from people in meetings and public forums that they believed it was better for racism to be out in the open, rather than concealed. It's a view usually stated with the certitude of a mathematical law. But not once—ever—has a person on the receiving end of racism confided in me that they were grateful for having been called a 'coon', 'curry-muncher', 'sand-nigger', or 'gook'. Not once have I heard such a person tell me they welcomed it, because it flushed bigotry out into the open, and gave them an opening to reform a bigot. Only in theory can you talk rationally with hate, intellectually shame a hater with your superior argument, and have their hatred magically reformed.

There's another problem with liberalism: its optimistic belief in progress lends to complacency. It wasn't that long ago that people were contemplating visions of a post-racial society. What that meant exactly, I always found unclear. But the aspiration was a tantalising one, at least, if it meant that racism was to be made a thing of the past.

Even today, there is still an air of optimism from some quarters. If hate and racism are being expressed right now, then maybe it's bigotry's riotous last gasp. After all, in so many parts of the West, the demographics are on the side of multiculturalism and tolerance. If we can see off the current tumult, there will be a safe path back to progress. Mind you, people were saying in 2016 that it was impossible for Trump to win the presidential election in the United States because the demographics weren't in his favour. Unexpected last gasp victories (or defeats) do happen.

Let's acknowledge that there's a chance we may be too hasty in declaring a crisis, that nationalist populism and illiberal democracy may not be existential threats. Believing the present to be re-enacting crises of the past may prevent us from seeing what is new about contemporary events. Moreover, democracies are often more resilient than they appear. Think about the turbulent politics of the 1960s and 70s, and the social divisions generated by the Vietnam War. Hate and polarisation were around then, too. It took time, but the wounds did heal.

The greater risk seems to be one of arrogance. As is often said, those who can't remember the past are condemned to repeat it.

Some of those who lived through the fascism of the twentieth century are in no doubt about the danger. Former US secretary of state Madeleine Albright, whose Jewish family fled Nazi-occupied Czechoslovakia as refugees, is one of them. She warns about another lapse into authoritarianism. As she writes, though, 'fascism rarely makes a dramatic entrance'.[42] Fascist political leaders can begin as seemingly minor characters, but have an uncanny ability to strike when the opportunity arises. The way fascism works is to use, at first, small aggressions, and build up to larger ones when met with no opposition.

When it has emerged, fascism doesn't always occur through a violent takeover of democracy. It can be enacted from within. Of the two most definitive fascist regimes, Mussolini's Italy and Hitler's Germany, Mussolini was invited by Italian monarch Victor Emmanuel III to form government in 1922, and Hitler was invited by German President von Hindenburg to become chancellor in 1933. This is how it happens: charismatic leaders of political parties, claiming to act in the name of the people, secure the office of government through constitutional means. But once there, they go after their opponents, persecute minorities, suspend rights and liberties, suppress the truth with propaganda, and wage war. By then, the ability of democracy to resist the pathogen has been fatally compromised.

Incipient fascism also thrives on complicity. In *The Origins of Totalitarianism*, the philosopher Hannah Arendt explained how the Nazi regime organised the German masses into total domination with such supreme efficiency because it understood the psychology of compliance. Its leaders understood that 'most people are neither bohemians, fanatics, adventurers, sex maniacs, crackpots, nor social failures, but first and foremost job holders and good family men'. The average person who was organised to carry out the gravest of crimes against humanity 'bore the features of the philistine rather than the mob man, and was the bourgeois who in the midst of the ruins of the world worried about nothing as much as his private security'.[43] Beware the indifferent citizen next door, the respectable neighbour who cares only about their mortgage.

Under certain conditions, and with the right actors, nationalist populism can be a prelude to fascism, rather than an episodic venting of cultural and racial anger. When the practitioners of populism play off 'the people' against 'the elites', and urge their followers to destroy all their supposed ene-mies, you can end up with more than just a bit of steam being let off. The whole engine of democracy can get blown up. What begins as hate of foreigners and minorities, and the resentment of the forgotten, ends up as ruthless state power wielded by dictators.

When you put it this way, it may sound alarmist to think that Australian democracy is vulnerable to such a threat. Unlike many of our liberal democratic cousins, we've not had to contend with the destabilising effects of an economic recession. We've had twenty-seven straight years of economic growth, as strong a bulwark as anything, you'd think, against liberal democratic decay.

Yet our democracy isn't in rude health. For a number of years, confidence has been draining out from democracy, especially among younger Australians. The Lowy Institute's annual poll of attitudes in 2018 found that only 49 per cent of people aged 18–29 and 45 per cent of people aged 30–44 agreed that democracy is the most preferable system of government. More than a quarter (26 per cent) of 18–29 year olds and more than a third (35 per cent) of 30–44 year olds agreed that, in some circumstances, non-democratic government may be preferable.[44] In the minds of so many, the door is already open to authoritarian rule.

I hope the optimists are proven right. Nothing is ever predestined. It's just that the conditions for a transition from populism to fascism appear to be emerging. The rapid nor-malisation of racial hatred is most worrying. When politicians give in to the temptations of demonising minorities and pitting groups against each other, this is where you end up.

The problem isn't just that some politicians have lost their bearings. Our conventional view of evil and hate is to see them as exceptional, instead of as things of which all of us are capable. But hate isn't an aberration. We all have it in us to hate, and we all can be conditioned to do it. It's something that can be built into democratic institutions, not only by politicians seeking advantage from fear-mongering, but also by communities themselves.

Hate is always latent, as a democracy requires a separation of 'us' and 'them'. This has long been the paradox of liberal democracy: equal rights are to be enjoyed by everyone, but not everyone is admitted into the community that confers those rights. In one sense, hate is what we see when a given community determines who counts as a member:

who is to be included as one of 'us', and who is to be excluded as one of 'them'. As much as we may want to, we can never escape or eradicate hate, but we must know how to live with it. The fight is as much with something out there—the barbarian forces of populism and extremism—as it is within liberal democracy itself. The best we can hope for is to civilise our attraction to it, and to overcome it in our moments of weakness.

Acknowledgements

Thanks to Louise Adler and Sally Heath for suggesting the idea of this essay, and to Catherine McInnis and Louise Stirling for their improvements to the text. Dennis Glover, Geoff Gallop, Gerald Ng, Nick Dyrenfurth and John Keane also provided helpful suggestions. Jeremy Spinak was a usual source of encouragement but sadly won't see the final product. Thanks most of all to Sarah and Danton.

Notes

1 William Hazlitt, 'On the Pleasure of Hating', in *The Plain Speaker: Opinions on Books, Men, and Things* London: Bell & Daldy, ([1821] 1870), p. 177.

2 For an overview of the psychology of hate, see Robert J Sternberg (ed.) *The Psychology of Hate*, Washington DC: American Psychological Association, 2005.

3 Friedrich Nietzsche, *On the Genealogy of the Morals: A Polemic*, (trans. M. Scarpitti), London: Penguin Books, 2013, p. 34.

4 Watkin Tench, *Watkin Tench's 1788* (ed. T. Flannery), Melbourne: Text Publishing, 2011, p. 91.

5 Henry Reynolds, *Forgotten War*, Sydney: NewSouth Publishing, 2013.

6 Paul Daley, 'Lachlan Macquarie was no humanitarian: his own words show he was a terrorist', *Guardian Australia*, 5 April 2016, https://www.theguardian.com/australia-news/postcolonial-blog/2016/apr/05/lachlan-macquarie-was-no-humanitarian-his-own-words-show-he-was-a-terrorist (viewed November 2018).

7 Ibid.

8 Charles Pearson, *National Life and Character: A Forecast*, London: Macmillan, 1893, pp. 84–5.

9 Alfred Deakin, *Commonwealth Parliamentary Debates*, House of Representatives (12 September 1901), p. 4807.

10 See Australian Bureau of Statistics, 2024.0 Census of Population and Housing: Australia Revealed, 2016, http://www.abs.gov.au/ausstats/abs@.nsf/mf/2024.0 (viewed November 2018); Australian Human Rights Commission et al., *Leading for Change: A Blueprint for Cultural Diversity and Inclusive Leadership Revisited*, Sydney: Australia Human Rights Commission, 2018, p. 7.

11 Australian Human Rights Commission, *Leading for Change*, p. 9.

12 For the leading account of whiteness in Australia, see Ghassan Hage, *White Nation: Fantasies of White Supremacy in a Multicultural Society*, Sydney: Pluto Press, 1998.

13 Megan Davis, 'Voice, Treaty, Truth', *The Monthly*, July 2018, https://www.themonthly.com.au/issue/2018/july/1530367200/megan-davis/voice-treaty-truth (viewed November 2018).

14 Paul Karp, 'Peter Dutton says Victorians scared to go out because of "African gang violence"', *Guardian*

Australia, 3 January 2018, https://www.theguardian.com/australia-news/2018/jan/03/peter-dutton-says-victorians-scared-to-go-out-because-of-african-gang-violence (viewed November 2018); Kathy Lord, 'Sudanese gangs a "real concern" in Melbourne, Prime Minister Malcolm Turnbull says', ABC News, 17 July 2018, https://www.abc.net.au/news/2018-07-17/sudanese-gangs-real-concern-in-melbourne-malcolm-turnbull-says/10002556 (viewed November 2018); Luke Henriques-Gomes, '"Nasty, bigoted": Victorian Liberals condemned for gang warning leaflets', *Guardian Australia*, 13 July 2018, https://www.theguardian.com/australia-news/2018/jul/13/victorian-liberals-defend-election-leaflets-warning-of-gangs-hunting-in-packs (viewed November 2018).

15 Amy Remeikis, 'Australia could add "values test" for migrants, Malcolm Turnbull says', *Guardian Australia*, 20 July 2018, https://www.theguardian.com/australia-news/2018/jul/20/australia-ethnic-segregation-minister-alan-tudge (viewed November 2018); Michael Koziol and Melissa Cunningham, '"There is a problem": Tony Abbott questions all African immigration amid gang violence debate', *Sydney Morning Herald*, 25 July 2018, https://www.smh.com.au/politics/federal/there-is-a-problem-tony-abbott-questions-all-african-immigration-amid-

gang-violence-debate-20180725-p4ztmh.html (viewed November 2018).

16 Malcolm Farr and Sam Clench, 'Government tries to explain away its support for "It's OK to be white" motion', News.com.au, 16 October 2018, https://www.news.com.au/national/politics/government-tries-to-explain-away-its-support-for-its-ok-to-be-white-motion/news-story/f951c0f92d3929d-6856636be6a35ad65 (viewed November 2018).

17 Alex Mann, 'Haircuts and hate: The rise of Australia's alt-right', *Background Briefing*, ABC RN, 14 October 2018, https://www.abc.net.au/radionational/programs/backgroundbriefing/haircuts-and-hate:-inside-the-rise-of-australias-alt-right/10365948 (viewed November 2018).

18 Andrew Bolt, 'Unity lost to the new tribe', *Herald Sun*, 2 August 2018, p. 13. For an example of Bolt's derision towards a non-discriminatory immigration policy, see Andrew Bolt, 'Who let them in?', *Herald Sun*, 19 November 2018, https://www.heraldsun.com.au/blogs/andrew-bolt/who-let-them-in/news-story/a6b88064020d0fbe979175598ec0cecf (viewed November 2018).

19 Osman Faruqi, 'Sky News Presenters Are Slamming Rowan Dean's Race-Based Attack On Tim Soutphommasane', *Junkee*, 11 July 2017, https://junkee.com/

sky-news-rowan-dean-tim-soutphommasane/112047 (viewed November 2018).

20 Paige Cockburn, 'Ross Cameron sacked by Sky News after making racist comments on Outsiders program', ABC News, 2 November 2018, https://www.abc.net.au/news/2018-11-02/ross-cameron-sacked-by-sky-news-after-making-racist-comments/10460992 (viewed November 2018).

21 Melissa Davey, 'Channel Seven under fire over interview with far-right activist', *Guardian Australia*, 15 January 2018, https://www.theguardian.com/australia-news/2018/jan/15/channel-seven-under-fire-interview-far-right-activist-blair-cottrell (viewed November 2018).

22 AAP, 'Pauline Hanson "not a welcome presence", says Turnbull', SBS World News, https://www.sbs.com.au/news/pauline-hanson-not-a-welcome-presence-says-turnbull (viewed November 2018).

23 Katharine Murphy, 'Sinodinos ducks query on preferencing One Nation above Nationals', *Guardian Australia*, 12 February 2017, https://www.theguardian.com/australia-news/2017/feb/12/arthur-sinodinos-bats-away-question-on-one-nation-preference-deal (viewed November 2018).

NOTES

24 Jacqueline Maley, 'Letting the far right in: how Jim Molan helped give extremism a respectable face', *Sydney Morning Herald*, 9 February 2018, https://www.smh.com.au/opinion/letting-the-far-right-in-how-jim-molan-helped-give-extremism-a-respectable-face-20180208-h0vsal.html (viewed November 2018).

25 JM Berger, 'Trump Is the Glue That Binds the Far Right', *The Atlantic*, October 2018, https://www.theatlantic.com/ideas/archive/2018/10/trump-alt-right-twitter/574219/ (viewed November 2018).

26 Angela Nagle, *Kill All Normies: The online culture wars from Tumblr and 4chan to the alt-right and Trump*, Winchester UK: Zero Books, 2017.

27 James Baldwin, 'The Fire Next Time', in *Collected Essays* (ed. T Morrison), New York: The Library of America, 1998, p. 299.

28 Cited in Robert Manne, 'The Howard Years: A Political Interpretation', in Robert Manne (ed.) *The Howard Years*, Melbourne: Black Inc, 2004, p. 16.

29 Heather Timmons, 'Stochastic terror and the cycle of hate that pushes unstable Americans to violence', *Quartz*, 27 October 2018, https://qz.com/1436267/trump-stochastic-terror-and-the-hate-that-ends-in-violence/ (viewed November 2018).

30 Emma Griffiths, 'George Brandis defends "right to be a bigot" amid Government plan to amend Racial Discrimination Act', ABC News, 24 March 2014, https://www.abc.net.au/news/2014-03-24/brandis-defends-right-to-be-a-bigot/5341552 (viewed November 2018).

31 Matthew Knott, 'Race-hate laws: silent majority speaks up', *Sydney Morning Herald*, 28 March 2017, p.1; Andrew Markus, *Mapping Social Cohesion: The Scanlon Foundation Surveys 2018*, Melbourne: Monash University, p. 64.

32 Jacqueline Maley, 'Exiting race commissioner blasts "weak" title change', *Sydney Morning Herald*, 12 June 2018, p. 3.

33 Martin Luther King Jr, 'Letter from a Birmingham Jail', 16 April 1963, *King Papers*, Martin Luther King Jr Research and Education Institute, Stanford University, pp. 10–11, okra.stanford.edu/transcript/document_images/undecided/630416-019.pdf (viewed November 2018).

34 Robin Di Angelo, *White Fragility: Why It's So Hard for White People to Talk About Racism*, Boston: Beacon Press, 2018.

35 Shannon Burns, 'In Defence of the Bad, White Working Class', *Meanjin*, Vol. 72, No. 2 (Winter 2017), p. 38.

36 Ta-Nehisi Coates, *We Were Eight Years in Power: An American Tragedy*, London: Hamish Hamilton, 2017, p. 343.

37 David Marr, 'The White Queen: One Nation and the Politics of Race', *Quarterly Essay* 65, Melbourne: Black Inc, 2017, p. 48.

38 Margo Kingston, 'Pauline Hanson takes centre stage again but this time we should listen not lampoon', *Guardian Australia*, 4 July 2016, https://www.theguardian.com/australia-news/2016/jul/04/pauline-hanson-takes-centre-stage-again-but-this-time-we-should-listen-not-lampoon (viewed November 2018).

39 Dwane Brown, 'How One Man Convinced 200 Ku Klux Klan Members To Give Up Their Robes', *NPR*, 20 August 2017, https://www.npr.org/2017/08/20/544861933/how-one-man-convinced-200-ku-klux-klan-members-to-give-up-their-robes (viewed November 2018).

40 Janet Albrechtsen, 'Wake up to hashtag assassins', *The Weekend Australian*, 24 November 2018, p. 21.

41 Aleksandar Hemon, 'Fascism is Not an Idea to Be Debated, It's a Set of Actions to Fight', *Literary Hub*, 1 November 2018, https://lithub.com/fascism-is-not-an-idea-to-be-debated-its-a-set-of-actions-to-fight/ (viewed November 2018).

NOTES

42 Madeleine Albright (with B Woodward), *Fascism: A Warning*, London: William Collins, 2018, p. 229.

43 Hannah Arendt, *The Origins of Totalitarianism*, New York: Harcourt, 1968, p. 338.

44 Alex Oliver, *Lowy Institute Poll 2018*, Sydney: Lowy Institute, 2018, p. 17.